THE ITALIAN RECIPES 2021

THE SECRETS OF ITALY'S BEST REGIONAL COOKS

SECOND EDITION

FISH, PAULTRY AND EASY DESSERTS

ANNA MELI

BUON

APPETITO

A TUTTI VOI!!!

TABLE OF CONTENTS

Fried Calamari

Calamari Fritti

Makes 6 to 8 servings

Many people outside of Italy don't really equate calamari with squid, something they may think they don't like. They just know they love "fried calamari," which are as irresistible as potato chips. In Italy, all along the coast, fried calamari are served alone or as part of a mixed fish fry with small shrimp, whitebait, and baby octopus.

In Sicily many years ago, I was served a plateful of tiny whole calamari fried this way. When I stuck my fork into one, I was shocked to find that the ink sac had not been removed and deep purple-black ink spurted all over my plate. It is fine to eat, though it was unexpected. Ink sacs are removed from calamari in the United States because the seafood keeps better without the sacs and can be frozen. (Most calamari sold here has been frozen.)

These calamari are lightly dusted with flour. It makes a thin, sheer coating when fried, and though it is crisp, the color barely changes.

2 pounds cleaned calamari (squid)

1 cup all-purpose flour

1 teaspoon salt

Freshly ground black pepper

Olive or vegetable oil for frying

1 lemon, cut into wedges

1. Make a small slit at the pointed end of each calamari. Rinse thoroughly, letting the water run through the body sac. Drain and pat dry. Cut the bodies crosswise into $1/2$-inch rings. If large, cut the base of each group of tentacles in half. Pat dry.

2. Spread the flour on a sheet of wax paper and season with salt and pepper. Line a tray with paper towels.

3. Pour oil to a depth of 2 inches in a deep heavy saucepan, or fill a deep-fryer according to the manufacturer's directions. Heat the oil to 370°F on a frying thermometer or until a small piece of the calamari placed in the oil sizzles and browns lightly in 1 minute.

4. When the correct temperature is reached, lightly roll a few pieces of calamari in the flour mixture. Shake off the excess flour. Slip the pieces into the hot oil with tongs without crowding the pan. Cook until the calamari turn lightly golden, about 3 minutes.

5. With a slotted spoon, transfer the calamari to the paper towels. Repeat with the remaining calamari. Sprinkle with salt. Serve hot with lemon wedges.

Venetian-Style Calamari

Calamari alla Veneta

Makes 4 Servings

In Venice, this is made with seppie, *cuttlefish and its ink. Because cuttlefish is hard to find, calamari (squid) is a good substitute. Most calamari here is sold with the ink sac removed, though many fish markets sell calamari or cuttlefish ink in little plastic envelopes. If it is available, add some of the ink to the sauce ingredients for a deep rich color and flavor. In Venice, fish is often served with* Polenta *made with white rather than yellow cornmeal.*

¼ olive oil

¼ cup finely chopped onion

2 whole garlic cloves

2 pounds calamari (squid), cleaned and cut into rings

2 medium tomatoes, peeled, seeded, and chopped, or 1 cup chopped canned tomatoes

½ cup dry white wine

Salt and freshly ground black pepper

1. Pour the oil into a large heavy skillet. Add the onion and garlic and cook over medium heat, stirring frequently, until the onion is golden, about 10 minutes. Discard the garlic.

2. Add the calamari, tomatoes, wine, and salt and pepper to taste. Bring to a simmer and cook until the sauce is thickened and the calamari are tender, about 30 minutes. Serve hot.

Calamari with Artichokes and White Wine

Calamari e Carciofi

Makes 4 servings

The sweetness of artichokes complements the flavor of several classic seafood recipes from Liguria. If you don't want to go to the trouble of cleaning fresh artichokes, you can substitute a package of frozen artichoke hearts.

1½ pounds cleaned calamari (squid)

4 medium artichokes

1 garlic clove, finely chopped

2 tablespoons chopped fresh flat-leaf parsley

¼ cup olive oil

1 cup dry white wine

Salt and freshly ground black pepper

1. Rinse the calamari thoroughly inside and out. Drain well. Cut the bodies crosswise into ¹/₂-inch rings. Cut the tentacles in half through the base. Pat dry.

2. Trim the artichokes, removing the stem end and all the outer leaves until you reach the pale green central cone. With a small knife, pare away any dark green patches from the base. Cut the artichokes in half and scrape away the fuzzy inner choke. Cut each half into thin slices.

3. Put the garlic, parsley, and oil in a large skillet over medium heat. Cook until the garlic is golden, about 1 minute. Stir in the calamari and salt to taste. Add the wine and bring to a simmer over low heat. Cover and cook 20 minutes.

4. Stir in the artichokes and 2 tablespoons water. Cook 30 minutes or until tender. Serve hot.

Grilled Stuffed Calamari

Calamari Ripieni

Makes 4 servings

Calamari are perfect for stuffing, but buy large calamari or the job will be tedious. Do not fill the body cavities more than half full. They shrink considerably as they cook, so the filling can burst out if they are overstuffed. This recipe is from Puglia in southern Italy.

8 to 12 large calamari (squid), about 6 to 8 inches long, cleaned

1 cup plain dry bread crumbs

¼ cup olive oil

2 tablespoons grated Pecorino Romano or Parmigiano-Reggiano

1 garlic clove, finely chopped

1 tablespoon chopped fresh flat-leaf parsley

Salt and freshly ground black pepper

1 lemon, cut into wedges

1. Make a small slit at the pointed end of each calamari. Rinse thoroughly, letting the water run through the body sac. Drain and pat dry.

2. Stir together the bread crumbs, oil, cheese, garlic, parsley, and salt and pepper to taste. Set aside $^1/_4$ cup of the mixture. Stuff the rest of the mixture loosely into the calamari, filling them only halfway. Tuck the tentacles into the body sac and secure them with wooden picks. Roll the calamari in the remaining bread crumb mixture.

3. Place a barbecue grill or broiler rack about 5 inches from the heat source. Preheat the grill or broiler.

4. Grill or broil the calamari until the bodies are opaque and lightly browned, about 2 minutes per side. Transfer to a platter and serve hot with lemon wedges.

Calamari Stuffed with Olives and Capers

Calamari Ripieni

Makes 4 servings

Calamari (squid) toughen quickly when they are heated, but they become tender when cooked in a liquid for at least 30 minutes. For the best texture, cook calamari quickly, grilling or frying them, or stew them slowly until they become tender, as in this recipe.

2½ pounds cleaned large calamari (squid), about 6 to 8 inches long

2 tablespoons olive oil

1 garlic clove, finely chopped

½ cup plain bread crumbs

2 tablespoons chopped fresh flat-leaf parsley

2 tablespoons chopped Gaeta or other mild black olives

2 tablespoons chopped, rinsed, and drained capers

½ teaspoon dried oregano, crumbled

Salt and freshly ground black pepper

Sauce

¼ cup olive oil

½ cup dry red wine

2 cups chopped canned peeled tomatoes with their juice

1 large garlic clove, lightly crushed

Pinch of crushed red pepper

Salt

1. Make a small slit at the pointed end of each calamari. Rinse thoroughly, letting the water run through the body sac. Drain and pat dry. Separate the bodies from the tentacles with a knife. Set the bodies aside. Chop the tentacles either with a large knife or in a food processor.

2. Pour the 2 tablespoons oil into a medium skillet. Add the garlic. Cook over medium heat until the garlic begins to turn golden, about 1 minute. Stir in the tentacles. Cook, stirring, for 2 minutes. Add the bread crumbs, parsley, olives, capers, and oregano. Add salt and pepper to taste. Remove from the heat and let cool.

3. With a small spoon, stuff the bread crumb mixture loosely into the calamari bodies, filling them only halfway. Secure the calamari with wooden toothpicks.

4. Choose a skillet large enough to hold all of the calamari in a single layer. Pour in the $1/4$ cup oil and heat over medium heat. Add the calamari and cook, turning them with tongs, until they are just opaque, about 2 minutes per side.

5. Add the wine and bring to a simmer. Stir in the tomatoes, garlic, crushed red pepper, and salt to taste. Bring to a simmer. Partially cover the pan and cook, turning the calamari occasionally, until they are very tender, 50 to 60 minutes. Add a little water if the sauce becomes too thick. Serve hot.

Stuffed Calamari, Roman Style

Calamari Ripieni alla Romana

Makes 4 servings

When I was studying Italian in Rome many years ago, I frequently had lunch at a family-run trattoria near the school. Every day the place would fill with workers from the nearby shops and office buildings who would pack the dining room clamoring for the home-style dishes they served. The menu was limited, but it was inexpensive and very good. This is my interpretation of their stuffed calamari.

1½ pounds cleaned large calamari (squid), about 6 to 8 inches long

1 cup plain dry bread crumbs

3 garlic cloves, finely chopped

2 tablespoons finely chopped fresh flat-leaf parsley

Salt and freshly ground black pepper

5 tablespoons olive oil

1 large onion, finely chopped

2 cups peeled, seeded, and chopped tomatoes

½ cup dry white wine

1. Make a small slit at the pointed end of each calamari. Rinse thoroughly, letting the water run through the body sac. Drain and pat dry. Finely chop the tentacles.

2. In a bowl, combine the tentacles, bread crumbs, garlic, parsley, and salt and pepper to taste. Add 2 to 3 tablespoons olive oil or enough to moisten the mixture. With a small spoon, stuff the bread crumb mixture loosely into the calamari, filling them only halfway. Secure the calamari with wooden toothpicks.

3. Pour the remaining 3 tablespoons oil into a large skillet. Add the onion. Cook over medium heat, stirring frequently, until tender, about 10 minutes. Stir in the tomatoes, wine, and salt and pepper to taste. Bring to a simmer, then reduce the heat to low. Add the calamari. Cover and cook, stirring occasionally, 50 to 60 minutes, or until the calamari are tender when pierced with a fork. Serve hot.

Mauro's Grilled Octopus with Fennel and Orange

Insalata di Polipo

Makes 4 servings

Fennel and orange salad is a classic Sicilian dish. In this creative recipe from my friend Chef Mauro Mafrici, the refreshing salad is topped by crisp grilled octopus. Be sure to slice the fennel as thin as possible, with a sharp knife, a mandoline, or the very fine blade of a food processor.

Octopus may look intimidating, but they need little effort to prepare. When cooked right, they are mild tasting and pleasantly chewy. Octopus is usually sold in supermarket fish departments or fish markets frozen or thawed. If purchased frozen, thaw it in a bowl of cold water, changing the water several times. This recipe is typically made with small octopus weighing about 6 ounces each. One large octopus can be substituted if the small ones are not available.

4 to 8 baby octopus, about 6 ounces each, or 1 large octopus, about 2½ pounds

5 tablespoons extra-virgin olive oil

1 garlic clove, finely chopped

2 tablespoons coarsely chopped flat-leaf parsley

Salt and freshly ground black pepper

1 medium fennel bulb

1 tablespoon freshly squeezed lemon juice, or to taste

2 or 3 navel oranges, peeled and sectioned

1 cup mild black olives, such as Gaeta

1. Check the base of the octopus to see if the hard, round beak has been removed. Squeeze it out if necessary. Bring a large saucepan of water to a boil. Add the octopus and simmer until tender when pierced with a knife, 30 to 60 minutes. Rinse and dry the octopus. Cut large octopus into 3-inch pieces.

2. In a bowl, combine the octopus with 3 tablespoons of the oil, the garlic, parsley, and a pinch of salt and pepper. Let marinate 1 hour up to overnight in the refrigerator

3. Slice off the base of the fennel and trim off any bruised spots. Remove the green stems, reserving the feathery green leaves, if any, for garnish. Cut the fennel into quarters lengthwise and trim away the core. Slice the quarters crosswise into very thin slices. You should have about 3 cups.

4. In a medium bowl, whisk the remaining 2 tablespoons of the oil, lemon juice, and salt to taste. Add the fennel, orange sections, olives, and fennel leaves, if available, and toss gently.

5. Place a barbecue grill rack or broiler pan about 4 inches from the heat. Preheat the grill or broiler. When ready, grill or broil the octopus, turning once, until browned and crisp, about 3 minutes per side.

6. Arrange the fennel salad on four plates and top with the octopus. Serve immediately.

Tomato-Braised Octopus

Polipetti in Salsa di Pomodoro

Makes 4

At one time, fishermen used to bash freshly caught octopus against the rocks to tenderize them. But today freezing and thawing them helps to break down the tough fibers. Simmering them in water, a Neopolitan method, ensures that they will be tender. Serve with lots of good bread to soak up the sauce.

4 to 8 baby octopus, about 6 ounces each, or 1 large octopus, about 2½ pounds

¼ cup olive oil

2 cups chopped canned peeled tomatoes with their juice

4 tablespoons chopped fresh flat-leaf parsley

2 large garlic cloves, finely chopped

Pinch of crushed red pepper

Salt

1. Check the base of the octopus to see if the hard, round beak has been removed. Squeeze it out if necessary. Bring a large saucepan of water to a boil. Add the octopus and simmer until tender when pierced with a knife, 30 to 60 minutes. Drain and dry the octopus, reserving some of the cooking liquid. Cut large octopus into bite-size pieces.

2. In a large heavy saucepan, heat the oil over medium heat. Add the octopus, tomatoes, 3 tablespoons of the parsley, the garlic, red pepper, and salt to taste. Stir to combine. Bring the sauce to a simmer. Cover the pot and cook over very low heat, stirring occasionally, for 30 minutes. Add a little of the reserved liquid if the sauce becomes too dry.

3. Uncover and cook 15 minutes more, or until the sauce is thick. Serve hot.

Conch Salad

Insalata di Scungilli

Makes 4 servings

On Christmas Eve, my family's table was always laden with a variety of fish and seafood—served in salads, baked, stuffed, sauced, and fried. My father's favorite was this salad made with conch or whelk—similar types of sea snails—though we always called it by its Neapolitan dialect name of scungilli.

Crunchy celery complements the slightly chewy seafood, though fresh fennel can be substituted.

1 pound fresh or frozen conch or whelk meat (scungilli)

Salt

⅓ cup extra-virgin olive oil

2 tender celery ribs

2 tablespoons chopped fresh flat-leaf parsley

1 garlic clove, finely chopped

Pinch of crushed red pepper

2 to 3 tablespoons fresh lemon juice

Radicchio or lettuce leaves

1. If using fresh conch, go to step 2. If the conch are frozen, place them in a bowl with cold water to cover. Put the bowl in the refrigerator at least 3 hours up to overnight, changing the water occasionally.

2. Bring a medium saucepan of water to a boil. Add the conch and 1 teaspoon salt. When the water returns to a simmer, cook the conch until tender when pierced with a fork, about 20 minutes. Drain and pat dry.

3. Begin cutting the conch into $1/4$-inch slices. When you come to a dark tube filled with a spongy matter, pull or cut it out and discard it, as it can be gritty. There is another tube on the outside of the body that does not need to be removed. Rinse the slices well and pat them dry.

4. In a medium bowl, combine the celery, parsley, garlic, red pepper, 2 tablespoons of the lemon juice, and a pinch of salt. Add the conch and taste for seasoning, adding the remaining lemon juice if needed.

5. Chill up to 1 hour or serve immediately on a bed of radicchio or lettuce leaves.

Conch in Hot Sauce

Scungilli in Salsa Piccante

Makes 6 to 8 servings

When I was a child my family used to go from our home in Brooklyn to Little Italy in downtown Manhattan for seafood. My father and uncles would order this dish, asking the waiter to make theirs extra-spicy. The seafood and sauce was spooned over freselle, *hard biscuits flavored with a lot of black pepper, which made the dish even hotter. My sister and cousins and I would, instead, share a plate of fried seafood or stuffed clams, never imagining we would one day enjoy such spicy food.*

Fresh conch or whelk (known in Italian as scungilli) is not easy to find in my area, so I use the kind that is partially precooked and frozen. It is available in most fish markets. I also use toasted bread. But if you like, freselle can be found in many Italian bakeries. Break them into pieces with your hands and sprinkle them with water to soften them up slightly.

2 pounds partially cooked fresh or frozen conch or whelk meat (scungilli)

⅓ cup olive oil

2 large garlic cloves, finely chopped

Pinch of crushed red pepper, or to taste

2 (28-ounce) cans peeled tomatoes, chopped

1 cup dry white wine

Salt

2 tablespoons chopped fresh flat-leaf parsley

Italian bread slices, toasted

1. If using fresh conch, go to step 2. If the conch are frozen, place them in a bowl with cold water to cover. Put the bowl in the refrigerator several hours or overnight, changing the water occasionally.

2. Begin cutting the conch into $1/4$-inch slices. When you come to a dark tube filled with a spongy matter, pull or cut it out and discard it, as it can be gritty. There is another tube on the outside of the body that does not need to be removed. Rinse the slices well and pat them dry.

3. Pour the oil into a large saucepan. Add the garlic and crushed red pepper. Cook over medium heat until the garlic is golden, about 2 minutes. Add the tomatoes and their juice, the wine, and salt to taste. Bring to a simmer. Cook 15 minutes on low heat, stirring occasionally.

4. Add the conch and bring to a simmer. Cook, stirring occasionally, until the conch is tender and the sauce is thickened, about 30 minutes. If the sauce becomes too thick, stir in a little water. Taste for seasoning, adding more pepper, if desired. Stir in the parsley.

5. Place slices of toasted Italian bread in the bottom of 4 pasta bowls. Spoon on the conch and serve immediately.

<u>MIXED SEAFOOD</u>

Seafood Couscous

Cuscusu

Makes 4 to 6 servings

Couscous dates back at least to the ninth century in Sicily, when the Arabs ruled the western portion of the island. At one time it was made by hand-rolling semolina into tiny pellets, but now it is available precooked (instant) in any grocery store. In the seaside town of Trapani, couscous is made with meat, fish, or vegetables. This is my version of the seafood couscous I tasted while visiting that area.

It's usually better to use fish broth with fish dishes, but you can also use chicken broth in a pinch; homemade is always preferred.

2 cups fish or <u>Chicken Broth</u>

2 cups water

1½ cups instant couscous

Salt

¼ cup olive oil

1 large onion, chopped

2 garlic cloves, very finely chopped

1 bay leaf

2 large tomatoes, peeled, seeded, and chopped, or 2 cups chopped canned tomatoes with the juice

4 tablespoons chopped fresh flat-leaf parsley

Pinch of ground cinnamon

Pinch of ground cloves

Pinch of freshly ground nutmeg

Pinch of saffron threads, crumbled

Pinch of ground cayenne

Salt and freshly ground black pepper

2 pounds assorted firm-fleshed fish fillets or steaks, such as swordfish, halibut, monkfish, or sea bass, and shellfish

1. Bring the broth and water to a boil. Place the couscous in a heat-proof bowl and stir in 3 cups of the liquid and salt to taste. Set the remaining liquid aside. Cover the couscous and let stand until the liquid is absorbed, about 10 minutes. Fluff the couscous with a fork.

2. Pour the oil into a pot large enough to hold the fish in a single layer. Add the onion and garlic. Cook over medium-low heat, stirring frequently, until tender, about 10 minutes. Add the bay leaf and cook 1 minute more. Add the tomatoes, 2 tablespoons of the parsley, the cinnamon, cloves, nutmeg, saffron, and cayenne. Cook for 5 minutes. Add 2 cups water and salt and pepper to taste. Bring to a simmer.

3. Meanwhile, remove any skin or bones from the fish. Cut the fish into 2-inch chunks.

4. Add the fish to the pot. Cover and cook 5 to 10 minutes, or until the fish is just barely opaque in the thickest part. With a slotted spoon, transfer the fish to a warm plate. Cover and keep warm.

5. Add the couscous to the pot. Cover and cook 5 minutes, or until hot. Taste and adjust seasoning. Add some of the reserved broth if the couscous seems dry.

6. Spoon the couscous onto a deep serving platter. Top with the fish. Sprinkle with the remaining parsley and serve immediately.

Mixed Fish Fry

Gran Fritto Misto di Pesce

Makes 4 to 6 servings

A thin coating of flour is all that is needed to make a light crust on small fish or cut-up pieces of calamari (squid). You can use this method for one type of fish or seafood, such as calamari, or use several varieties.

4 ounces cleaned calamari (squid)

1 pound very small fresh fish, such as whitebait, fresh (not canned) anchovies, or sardines, cleaned

4 ounces small shrimp, shelled and deveined

1 cup all-purpose flour

1 teaspoon salt

Vegetable oil for frying

1 lemon, cut into wedges

1. Rinse the calamari and drain well. Cut the bodies into $^1/_2$-inch rings. If large, cut each group of tentacles in half through the base. Removing the heads from small whole fish such as anchovies or sardines is optional. Whitebait are always left whole. Rinse the fish thoroughly inside and out. Pat dry.

2. Stir together the flour and salt on a piece of wax paper, then spread it out.

3. Line a tray with paper towels. In a deep heavy saucepan, pour enough oil to reach a depth of 2 inches, or if using an electric deep-fryer, follow the manufacturer's directions. Heat the oil to 370°F on a deep-frying thermometer, or until a 1-inch piece of bread dropped into the oil sizzles and browns in 1 minute.

4. Toss a small handful of the fish and shellfish in the flour mixture. Shake off the excess. Using tongs, carefully slip the fish into the hot oil. Do not crowd the pan. Fry until crisp and lightly golden, about 2 minutes.

5. With a slotted spoon, transfer the fish to the paper towels to drain. Keep warm in a low oven. Cook the remaining seafood in the same way. Serve hot with lemon wedges.

Molise-Style Fish Stew

Zuppa di Pesce alla Marinara

Makes 6 servings

Molise-style fish stew differs from that of other regions because of the presence of a large amount of sweet green peppers. Use the long Italian frying peppers or green bell peppers. Ideally you would make this with as wide a variety of fish as possible, but I have made it with only calamari (squid) and monkfish and it was very good. Molise cooks might use lobster, octopus, and rockfish or other firm-fleshed varieties.

¼ cup olive oil

1½ pounds Italian frying peppers, seeded and chopped

1 onion, chopped

Salt

2 tablespoons red wine vinegar

½ pound calamari (squid), cut into rings

1 pound firm whitefish steaks or fillets, cut into 2-inch chunks

½ pound medium shrimp, shelled, deveined, and cut into ½-inch pieces

2 tablespoons chopped fresh flat-leaf parsley

6 to 12 slices of Italian bread, toasted

Extra-virgin olive oil

1. In a large saucepan, heat the oil over medium heat. Stir in the peppers, onion, and salt to taste. Cover and reduce the heat to low. Cook, stirring occasionally, until very tender, about 40 minutes. Remove from the heat and let cool.

2. Scrape the contents of the pan into a food processor or blender. Process until smooth. Add the vinegar and salt to taste and process again briefly to blend.

3. Scrape the pepper and onion mixture back into the saucepan. Add 1 to 2 cups water or enough to make the liquid as thick as heavy cream. Bring it to a simmer over medium-low heat. Add the calamari and cook until tender when pierced with a fork, about 20 minutes.

4. Add the fish chunks and the shrimp. Cook until the fish is just cooked, about 5 minutes. Stir in the parsley. Serve hot with toasted bread and a drizzle of extra-virgin olive oil.

Poultry

Italian cooks have a wide range of poultry to choose from. In addition to chicken and turkey, capon, pheasant, guinea hen, duck, goose, pigeon, quail, and other birds are readily available.

Until after World War II, chicken was not widely eaten in Italy. Poultry was expensive, and a live chicken could produce eggs for a farm family either to eat or sell. Chickens were killed only when they became too old to lay eggs, when someone in the family was ill and needed extra nourishment, or for special feasts. Many of today's recipes for chicken were once made with wild birds or with rabbit.

For Christmas and other holidays, Italians often serve capon. The flavor of capon is similar to chicken, though deeper and richer. Roasted capon with a meat or bread stuffing is eaten all over Italy. In Emilia-Romagna, capons are roasted and stuffed or boiled to make broth in which to cook tiny hand-formed tortellini. One traditional recipe from the Veneto is capon cut into pieces, seasoned with herbs, and steamed in a pig's bladder to hold in the flavors. In Piedmont, capons are stuffed with truffles and boiled or roasted for holiday meals. A small turkey or large roasting chicken can be substituted for capon, if preferred.

Most of the recipes in this chapter are for chicken and turkey because the supply of those in the United States is reliable and consistent. For good chicken and turkey flavor, I prefer to use free-range poultry raised without antibiotics. Though organic and free-range birds are more expensive, they taste better, have a better texture, and are better for you.

No matter which type of poultry you will be cooking, remove the giblets, liver, and any other parts packed inside the cavity or in the neck area. Rinse the bird well inside and out. Occasionally, you will see still-attached pinfeathers, which should be removed, either with your fingers or with tweezers. Some types of poultry, such as chicken, capon, and duck, have excess fat that can be pulled or cut out of the cavity. If the bird will be cooked whole, bend the wing tips behind the back. Insert any stuffing or flavoring ingredients, then tie the legs together with kitchen string for a neat appearance and more even cooking.

Some chickens, turkeys, and other large birds come with a small thermometer inserted in the breast. These devices are often inaccurate, as they can become clogged with cooking juices. It is best to rely on an instant-read thermometer to check for doneness. Chicken, turkey, and capon are done when the juices run clear when the thigh is pierced with a fork and the temperature in the thickest part of the thigh is 170° to 175°F (for capon, 180°F) on an instant-read thermometer. Be sure that the thermometer does not touch the bone (or the temperature may read higher than that of the meat). Quail, goose, and duck are eaten well done in Italy, with the exception of duck breast. When pan cooked, duck breast is usually served medium rare.

CHICKEN CUTLETS (SCALOPPINE)

Scaloppine are thin, boneless, skinless slices of meat or poultry, usually called cutlets in English. They can be made from any type of meat and sometimes even firm-fleshed fish, but in the United States veal, chicken, and turkey are the most common. Though not the most flavorful cuts, scaloppine or cutlets are tender, cook rapidly, and take well to a variety of flavorings, so they are a good choice for quick meals.

Veal scaloppine are the most typical of Italian cooking, but good veal is expensive and not always readily available, so many cooks in the United States use chicken or turkey cutlets.

When purchasing chicken cutlets, look for whole, well-trimmed slices. At home, check to see that the slices are thin enough, no more than $1/4$ inch is best.

If the meat is thicker or unevenly cut, place the slices between two sheets of wax paper or plastic wrap. Pound them very gently with a smooth object such as a meat mallet. An inexpensive rubber plumber's mallet from the hardware store does a good job. Do not use a mallet with a craggy surface designed to break down fibers and tenderize meat, and do not pound too heavily or you will have finely chopped meat instead of thin, flat cutlets.

Chicken Cutlets Francese

Pollo alla Francese

Makes 4 servings

Many Italian-American restaurants used to feature these cutlets in a light, eggy crust with a lemon sauce. I don't know why it is called Francese, *meaning "French-style," but it might be because it was thought to be elegant. It is still a favorite and tastes great with buttery peas or spinach.*

1¼ pounds thin-sliced chicken cutlets

Salt and freshly ground black pepper

2 large eggs

½ cup all-purpose flour

½ cup Chicken Broth or store-bought

¼ cup dry white wine

2 to 3 tablespoons fresh lemon juice

3 tablespoons olive oil

3 tablespoons unsalted butter

1 tablespoon fresh flat-leaf parsley

1 lemon, cut into wedges

1. Place the chicken slices between two sheets of plastic wrap. Gently pound the slices to about $1/4$-inch thickness. Sprinkle the chicken with salt and pepper.

2. In a shallow bowl, beat the eggs with salt and pepper until well blended. Spread the flour on a piece of wax paper. Mix together the broth, wine, and lemon juice.

3. In a large skillet, heat the oil with the butter over medium heat until the butter melts. Dip only enough of the cutlets in the flour as will fit in the pan in a single layer. Then dip them in the egg.

4. Arrange the slices in the pan in a single layer. Cook the chicken until golden brown on the bottom, 2 to 3 minutes. Turn the chicken with tongs and brown on the other side, 2 to 3 minutes more. Regulate the heat so that the butter does not burn. Transfer the chicken to a plate. Cover with foil and keep warm. Repeat with the remaining chicken.

5. When all of the chicken is done, add the broth mixture to the pan. Raise the heat and cook, scraping the pan, until the sauce is slightly thickened. Stir in the parsley. Return the chicken pieces to the skillet and turn them once or twice in the sauce. Serve immediately with lemon wedges.

Chicken Cutlets with Basil and Lemon

Scaloppine di Pollo al Basilico e Limone

Makes 4 servings

Italians say, "That which grows together, goes together," and that is certainly true of lemons and basil. I had this elegant yet quick and easy dish at the very beautiful Hotel Quisisana on the island of Capri off the coast of Naples. Serve it with buttered spinach or asparagus and a bottle of falanghina, a flavorful white wine from the region of Campania.

1¼ pounds thin-sliced chicken or turkey cutlets

Salt and freshly ground black pepper

3 tablespoons unsalted butter

1 tablespoon olive oil

2 tablespoons fresh lemon juice

12 fresh basil leaves, stacked and cut into thin strips

1. Place the chicken slices between two sheets of plastic wrap. Gently pound the slices to about $1/4$-inch thickness. Sprinkle the chicken well with salt and pepper.

2. In a large heavy skillet, melt 2 tablespoons of the butter with oil. When the butter is melted, add as many chicken pieces as will fit without touching. Cook the chicken until golden brown, about 4 minutes. Turn the chicken and brown the other side, about 3 minutes more. Transfer the pieces to a plate. Repeat with the remaining chicken, if necessary.

3. Remove the pan from the heat. Add the remaining butter, the lemon juice, and the basil to the skillet and swirl it gently to melt the butter. Return the chicken pieces to the skillet and place it over the heat. Turn the chicken pieces once or twice in the sauce. Serve immediately.

Chicken Cutlets with Sage and Peas

Scaloppine di Pollo al Piselli

Makes 4 servings

Here chicken cutlets are married with sage and peas, and it looks as great as it tastes. If you are using frozen peas and don't have time to partially thaw them, just drop the peas into boiling water for 1minute, or rinse or soak them in very hot water. Drain them well before proceeding.

1¼ pounds thin-sliced chicken cutlets

Salt and freshly ground black pepper

2 tablespoons unsalted butter

2 tablespoons olive oil

12 fresh sage leaves

2 cups shelled fresh peas or partially thawed frozen peas

1 to 2 tablespoons fresh lemon juice

1. Place the chicken slices between two sheets of plastic wrap. Gently pound the slices to about $1/4$-inch thickness. Sprinkle the chicken well with salt and pepper.

2. In a large skillet, melt the butter with the olive oil over medium heat. Pat the chicken dry. Add the chicken and sage to the pan. Cook the chicken until golden brown, about 4 minutes. Turn the pieces with tongs and brown the other side, about 3 minutes more. Transfer the pieces to a plate.

3. Add the peas and lemon juice to the skillet and stir well. Add salt and pepper to taste. Cover and cook 5 minutes, or until the peas are almost tender.

4. Return the chicken pieces to the skillet and cook, turning them once or twice, until heated through. Serve hot.

Chicken with Gorgonzola and Walnuts

Petti di Pollo con Gorgonzola

Makes 4 servings

Gorgonzola is a creamy cow's milk blue cheese from the region of Lombardy. The cheese is creamy-white streaked with blue-green veins of an edible type of penicillin mold. Gorgonzola melts beautifully, and cooks in this region use it to make sauces for pasta and meat. Here it forms a delicious sauce for cutlets. A sprinkling of chopped walnuts gives the dish an added crunch. Serve the chicken with sautéed mushrooms and fresh broccoli.

1¼ pounds thin-sliced chicken cutlets

½ cup all-purpose flour

Salt and freshly ground black pepper

2 tablespoons unsalted butter

1 tablespoon olive oil

¼ cup finely chopped shallots

½ cup dry white wine

4 ounces gorgonzola, rind removed

2 tablespoons walnuts, coarsely chopped and toasted

1. Place the chicken slices between two sheets of plastic wrap. Gently pound the slices to about $1/4$-inch thickness. On a piece of wax paper, combine the flour and salt and pepper, to taste. Dip the chicken cutlets in the mixture. Shake to remove the excess.

2. In a large skillet over medium heat, melt the butter with the oil. Add the chicken and cook until golden brown, about 4 minutes. Turn the pieces with tongs and brown the other side, about 3 minutes more. Remove the chicken to a plate and keep warm.

3. Add the shallots to the skillet and cook for 1 minute. Stir in the wine and cook, scraping the bottom of the pan, until slightly thickened, about 1 minute. Reduce the heat to low. Return the chicken pieces to the skillet and turn them once or twice in the sauce.

4. Cut the cheese into slices and place them on top of the chicken. Cover and cook just until slightly melted, 1 to 2 minutes.

5. Sprinkle with the walnuts and serve immediately.

Salad-Topped Chicken Cutlets

Scaloppine di Pollo a l'Insalata

Makes 4 servings

At a favorite restaurant in New York called Dal Barone, large chicken cutlets fried in bread crumbs with a crunchy salad topping were called orecchie di elefante, *"elephant's ears." Though the restaurant closed several years ago, I still make my version of their chicken cutlets. Serve with ripe pears and cheese for dessert.*

1¼ pounds thin-sliced chicken cutlets

2 large eggs

½ cup freshly grated Parmigiano-Reggiano

2 tablespoons chopped fresh flat-leaf parsley

Salt and freshly ground black pepper

1 to 2 tablespoons all-purpose flour

¼ cup olive oil

Salad

2 tablespoons extra-virgin olive oil

1 to 2 tablespoons balsamic vinegar

Salt and freshly ground black pepper

4 cups mixed salad greens, torn into bite-size pieces

¼ cup thinly sliced red onion

1 medium ripe tomato, diced

1. Place the chicken cutlets between two sheets of plastic wrap. Gently pound the cutlets to a $1/4$-inch thickness.

2. In a medium bowl, beat the eggs with the cheese, parsley, and salt and pepper to taste. Beat in enough flour to make a smooth paste just thick enough to coat the chicken. Line a plate or tray with paper towels.

3. In a large skillet over medium heat, heat the $1/4$ cup of olive oil until a drop of the egg mixture sizzles when added.

4. Dip the cutlets in the egg mixture until well coated. Place just enough of the cutlets in the pan to fit comfortably in a single layer. Cook until browned, about 4 minutes. Turn the chicken with tongs and brown the other side, about 3 minutes more.

Drain on the paper towels. Transfer to a plate, cover with foil, and keep warm. Cook the remaining cutlets in the same way.

5. In a large bowl, whisk the 2 tablespoons olive oil, the vinegar, and salt and pepper to taste. Add the salad ingredients and toss well.

6. Top the cutlets with the salad and serve immediately.

Chicken Rolls with Anchovy Sauce

Involtini con Salsa di Acciughe

Makes 4 servings

Anchovies give a zesty flavor to the sauce on these easy chicken rolls. If you don't want to use anchovies, substitute some chopped capers.

¼ cup unsalted butter

4 anchovy fillets, drained and chopped

1 tablespoon chopped fresh flat-leaf parsley

¼ teaspoon freshly grated lemon zest

8 thin-sliced chicken cutlets

Freshly ground black pepper

8 thin slices imported Italian prosciutto

1. Place a rack in the center of the oven. Preheat the oven to 400°F. Butter a small pan.

2. In a small saucepan, melt the butter with the anchovies over medium heat, mashing the anchovies with the back of a spoon. Stir in the parsley and lemon zest. Set the sauce aside.

3. Place the chicken slices between two sheets of plastic wrap. Gently pound the slices to about $1/4$-inch thickness. Lay the chicken slices on a flat surface. Sprinkle with pepper. Place a piece of prosciutto on each slice. Roll up the slices lengthwise. Place the rolls in the pan seam-side down.

4. Drizzle the sauce over the chicken. Bake 20 to 25 minutes or until the juices run clear when the chicken is cut in the thickest part. Serve hot.

Chicken Rolls in Red Wine

Rollatini di Pollo al Vino Rosso

Makes 4 servings

Red wine colors these rolled chicken breasts from Tuscany a deep burgundy and makes a delicious sauce. Garlic, herbs, and thin slices of prosciutto is the typical filling. Though prosciutto from Parma is very good and the best-known variety in the United States, other types from outside the Parma area, such as prosciutto San Daniele, from Friuli, are now available, and though subtly different they are equally good.

The most important thing is to find a good source for prosciutto. The clerks should know how to slice the meat very thinly without shredding it and how to lay the slices out carefully on wax paper so that they do not stick together.

1 tablespoon chopped fresh rosemary

1 tablespoon chopped fresh sage

1 garlic clove, very finely chopped

8 thin-sliced chicken cutlets

Salt and freshly ground black pepper

8 slices imported Italian prosciutto

2 tablespoons olive oil

1 cup dry red wine

1. In a small bowl, combine the rosemary, sage, and garlic.

2. Lay the cutlets out on a flat surface. Sprinkle with the herb mixture and salt and pepper to taste. Place a slice of prosciutto on top. Roll up the cutlets lengthwise and tie them with kitchen string.

3. In a large skillet, heat the oil over medium heat. Add the chicken and cook, turning the pieces frequently with tongs, until browned on all sides, about 10 minutes.

4. Add the wine and cook, turning the pieces occasionally, until the chicken is cooked through and the juices run clear when cut in the thickest part, about 15 minutes.

5. Transfer the chicken rolls to a serving platter. Pour the sauce over them and serve immediately.

CHICKEN PARTS

"Devil's" Chicken

Pollo alla Diavola

Makes 4 servings

Tiny hot red chilies are called peperoncini, *"little peppers," in some regions and* diavolicchi, *"little devils," in others. The presence of crushed red pepper accounts for the Tuscan name for this chicken.*

I like to use cut-up chicken pieces for this dish. That way I can cook the legs and thighs a little longer than the more delicate wings and breasts.

1 chicken (about 3 pounds), cut into 8 serving pieces

⅓ cup freshly squeezed lemon juice

¼ cup olive oil

A generous pinch of crushed red pepper

Salt

1. With a chef's knife or poultry shears, remove the wing tips from the chicken.

2. In a large shallow dish, combine the lemon juice, oil, red pepper, and salt to taste. Add the chicken pieces. Cover and marinate at room temperature for 1 hour, turning the pieces occasionally.

3. Arrange a grill rack or broiler pan about 5 inches from the heat source. Preheat the grill or broiler.

4. When ready to cook, remove the chicken from the marinade and pat it dry. Place the chicken with the skin side toward the source of the heat. Grill or broil, basting occasionally with the marinade, until nicely browned, about 10 to 15 minutes. Turn the chicken and cook until the chicken juices run clear when the thigh is pierced with a knife in the thickest part, about 10 to 15 minutes more. Serve hot.

Crusty Broiled Chicken

Pollo Rosolato

Makes 4 servings

Chicken in a crisp bread crumb and cheese coating tastes great when just cooked and hot, but it is also good served cold the next day. Plan an Italian picnic with this chicken, Sweet and Sour Potatoes, Green Bean Salad, and sliced tomatoes.

1 chicken (about 3½ pounds), cut into serving pieces

Salt and freshly ground black pepper

½ cup plain dry bread crumbs

2 tablespoons freshly grated Parmigiano-Reggiano

1 large garlic clove, finely chopped

½ teaspoon dried oregano, crumbled

About 2 tablespoons olive oil

1. Place a broiler rack about 5 inches away from the heat source. Preheat the broiler.

2. Pat the chicken dry. Sprinkle with salt and pepper. Place the chicken skin-side down on the rack. Broil the chicken until lightly browned, about 10 minutes. Turn the chicken and cook 10 minutes more.

3. While the chicken is cooking, in a medium bowl, combine the bread crumbs, cheese, garlic, oregano, and salt and pepper to taste. Add just enough of the oil to make a thick paste.

4. Remove the broiler pan from the broiler. Set the oven heat to 350°F.

5. Coat the skin side of the chicken with the bread crumb mixture, patting it so that it adheres. Place the pan on the center rack of the oven and bake about 10 to 15 minutes more, until the juices run clear when the chicken is pierced with a knife in the thickest part of the thigh, and the crust is nicely browned. Serve hot or at room temperature.

Marinated Grilled Chicken

Pollo alla Griglia

Makes 4 servings

Vinegar, garlic, and herbs—typical ingredients of the Naples area, where my father's family was from—were always included in a marinade for whatever he was barbecuing. Usually the herb was mint, either fresh home-grown or dried, though sometimes he substituted fresh parsley or dried oregano. He used it on chicken, bluefish, and steak, and the results were always delicious.

Because the acid in the vinegar can actually "cook" any protein-rich food it comes in contact with, do not marinate tender fish for more than 30 minutes. Chicken and beef can marinate longer and will pick up more of the marinade flavor as they do.

½ cup red wine vinegar

2 large garlic cloves, chopped

2 tablespoons chopped fresh mint or flat-leaf parsley or 1 teaspoon dried oregano, crumbled

Salt and freshly ground black pepper

1 chicken (about 3½ pounds), cut into 8 serving pieces

1. In a shallow nonreactive dish, whisk together the vinegar, garlic, herb, and salt and pepper to taste. Add the chicken pieces. Cover and refrigerate for several hours up to overnight.

2. Place a barbecue grill or broiler rack about 5 inches away from the heat source. Preheat the grill or broiler.

3. Remove the chicken from the marinade. Pat the chicken dry. Place the chicken with the skin side toward the source of the heat. Grill or broil 12 to 15 minutes or until nicely browned. Turn the chicken and cook 10 to 15 minutes more, or until the chicken juices run clear when the chicken thigh is pierced with a knife in the thickest part. Serve hot or at room temperature.

Baked Chicken with Potatoes and Lemon

Pollo al Forno con Patate e Limone

Makes 4 servings

One of my favorite restaurants on the island of Capri is Da Paolino, set within a lemon grove. One evening my husband and I were enjoying a quiet, candlelit dinner when suddenly a fat ripe lemon from the tree above us crashed down into a glass, splashing water all over the table.

I think of that incident every time I make this lemony chicken. It is a typical home-style dish made all over southern Italy, where citrus is plentiful.

2 medium lemons

1 tablespoon olive oil

1 tablespoon chopped rosemary

2 garlic cloves, chopped

Salt and freshly ground black pepper

1 chicken (about 3½ pounds) cut into 8 serving pieces

1 pound all-purpose potatoes, peeled and cut into eighths

1. Place a rack in the center of the oven. Preheat the oven to 450°F. Oil a baking pan large enough to hold all of the ingredients in a single layer.

2. Cut one lemon into thin slices. Squeeze the juice of the remaining lemon into a medium bowl.

3. Add to the bowl the oil, rosemary, garlic, and salt and pepper to taste and whisk until combined.

4. Rinse the chicken pieces and pat dry. Place the chicken in the pan. Pour the lemon juice mixture over the chicken, turning the pieces to coat all sides. Arrange the chicken pieces skin side up. Tuck the potatoes and lemon slices around the chicken.

5. Bake the chicken for 45 minutes. Baste with the pan juices. Continue to bake, basting occasionally, 15 minutes more or until the chicken is browned and the potatoes are tender.

6. Transfer the contents of the pan to a serving platter. Pour the juices over the chicken and serve.

Country-Style Chicken and Vegetables

Pollo alla Paesana

Makes 4 servings

Some years ago, I visited Emilia-Romagna to learn about how Parmigiano-Reggiano is produced. I visited a dairy where the owner showed me how cheese was made daily. After a tour and cheesemaking lesson, my host invited me to join his family and coworkers for lunch. As we stepped into the big farmhouse kitchen, his wife was just removing large pans of chicken and vegetables from the oven. We nibbled on homemade salami and the typical crab-shaped white bread of the region known as coppia—"couple" *bread—because it is made in two sections that are joined together. Dessert was as simple as can be, wedges of ripe juicy pears and moist, aged Parmigiano.*

A baking pan large enough to hold all of the chicken and vegetables in a single layer is essential for this dish, or the ingredients will steam and not brown properly. If you don't have one large enough, use two smaller pans, dividing the ingredients evenly between them.

Vary this dish according to the vegetables in season and what you have on hand. Cut-up turnips, squash, or peppers can be added, or try a handful of cherry tomatoes.

½ to 1 cup homemade <u>Chicken Broth</u>, or store-bought

4 large garlic cloves, finely chopped

2 tablespoons chopped fresh flat-leaf parsley

2 tablespoons chopped fresh rosemary

¼ cup olive oil

Salt and freshly ground black pepper

1 (10-ounce) package white mushrooms, halved or quartered if large

6 medium boiling potatoes, peeled and cut into eighths

2 medium carrots, cut into 1-inch chunks

1 medium onion, cut into eighths

1 chicken (about 3½ pounds), cut into 8 serving pieces

1. Prepare the chicken broth, if necessary. Place a rack in the center of the oven. Preheat the oven to 450°F. Choose a baking pan large enough to hold all of the ingredients in a single layer, or use two pans. Oil the pan or pans.

2. Place the garlic, parsley, and rosemary in a small bowl and mix with the oil. Add salt and pepper to taste.

3. Scatter the mushrooms, potatoes, carrots, and onions in the pan. Add half the herb mixture and toss well. Brush the remaining herb mixture over the chicken pieces. Place the chicken skin-side up in the pan, arranging the vegetables around them.

4. Bake for 45 minutes. Baste the chicken with the pan juices. If the chicken seems dry, add a little of the chicken broth. Continue to bake, basting occasionally, 15 minutes more, or until the chicken juices run clear when pierced in the thickest part of the thigh with a knife and the potatoes are tender. If the chicken is not brown enough, run the pans under the broiler for 5 minutes or until the skin is browned and crisp.

5. Transfer the chicken and vegetables to a serving platter. Tip the pan and skim off the fat with a large spoon. Place the pan over medium heat. Add about $^1/_2$ cup of the chicken broth and scrape the bottom of the pan. Bring the juices to a simmer and cook until slightly reduced, about 5 minutes.

6. Pour the juices over the chicken and vegetables and serve immediately.

Chicken with Lemon and White Wine

Pollo allo Scarpariello I

Makes 4 servings

Scarpariello *means "shoemaker's style," and there are many theories
about how the name for this recipe came about. Some say little bits
of chopped garlic resemble the nailheads in a shoe, while others say
it was a quick dish a busy shoemaker cobbled together. Most likely, it
is an Italian-American invention, given an Italian name by a clever
restaurateur.*

*There are many versions of this dish, and every one I have tasted has
been delicious. Typically, the chicken is chopped into small chunks,
known as* spezzatino, *from* spezzare, *"to chop," so that the pieces
can absorb more of the tasty sauce. You can do this at home with a
cleaver or heavy knife, or have the butcher prepare the chicken for
you. If you prefer, you can simply cut the chicken at the joints into
serving-size pieces.*

1 chicken (about 3½ pounds)

Salt and freshly ground black pepper

3 tablespoons olive oil

2 tablespoons unsalted butter

3 large garlic cloves, finely chopped

3 tablespoons fresh lemon juice

¾ cup dry white wine

¼ cup chopped fresh flat-leaf parsley

1. Trim off the chicken wing tips and tail. Set them aside for another use. With a large heavy knife or cleaver, cut up the chicken at the joints. Cut the breasts, thighs, and legs into 2-inch chunks. Rinse the pieces and pat dry. Sprinkle all over with salt and pepper.

2. Heat the oil in a 12-inch skillet over medium-high heat. Add the chicken pieces in a single layer. Cook, turning the pieces occasionally, until nicely browned, about 15 to 20 minutes.

3. Lower the heat to medium. Spoon off the fat. Place the butter in the pan, and when it is melted, add the garlic. Turn the chicken pieces in the butter and add the lemon juice.

4. Add the wine and bring to a simmer. Cover and cook, turning the pieces occasionally, until the chicken juices run clear when

pierced with a knife in the thickest part of the thigh, about 10 minutes.

5. If there is a lot of liquid remaining, remove the chicken to a serving platter and keep warm. Turn the heat to high and boil until the liquid is reduced and slightly thickened. Stir in the parsley and pour over the chicken.

Chicken with Sausages and Pickled Peppers

Pollo allo Scarpariello II

Makes 6 servings

Chicken scarpariello probably became popular here before World War II, when many Italian immigrants to this country opened restaurants in big city neighborhoods known as Little Italy. Few were professional cooks, and many of the dishes they served were based on home cooking enhanced by the bounty of ingredients they found in this country.

Here is a second version of shoemaker's-style chicken. With sausage, vinegar, and pickled peppers, it is completely different from the <u>Chicken with Lemon and White Wine</u> recipe. And there are many other versions as well. No matter what its origins, chicken scarpariello is delicious and satisfying.

¼ cup homemade <u>Chicken Broth</u>, or store-bought

1 chicken (about 3½ pounds)

1 tablespoon olive oil

1 pound Italian-style pork sausage, cut into 1-inch chunks

Salt and freshly ground black pepper

6 large garlic cloves, thinly sliced

1 cup jarred pickled sweet peppers, cut into bite-size pieces

¼ cup pickling liquid from the peppers, or white wine vinegar

1. Prepare the chicken broth, if necessary. Trim off the chicken wing tips and tail. Set them aside for another use. With a large heavy knife or cleaver, cut up the chicken at the joints. Cut the breasts, thighs, and legs into 2-inch chunks. Rinse the pieces and dry well.

2. Heat the oil over medium high heat in a skillet large enough to hold all of the ingredients. Add the sausages pieces and brown well on all sides, about 10 minutes. Transfer the pieces to a plate.

3. Place the chicken pieces in the pan. Sprinkle with salt and pepper. Cook, stirring occasionally, until golden, about 15 minutes. Scatter the garlic around the chicken and cook 2 to 3 minutes more.

4. Tip the pan and spoon off most of the fat. Add the sausages, the broth, the peppers, and the pepper liquid or vinegar. Turn the heat to high. Cook, stirring the pieces often and basting them

with the liquid, until the liquid is reduced and forms a light glaze, about 15 minutes. Serve immediately.

Chicken with Celery, Capers, and Rosemary

Pollo alla Cacciatora Siciliana

Makes 4 servings

This is a Sicilian version of alla cacciatora, *"hunter's wife's" chicken. Celery is a nice touch, giving the sauce a little crunch. Sicilians often make this with rabbit.*

2 tablespoons olive oil

1 chicken (about 3½ pounds), cut into 8 pieces

Salt and freshly ground black pepper

⅓ cup red wine vinegar

½ cup chopped celery

¼ cup capers, rinsed and chopped

1 sprig fresh rosemary

1. Heat the oil in a large skillet over medium heat. Pat the chicken dry with paper towels. Add the chicken pieces and salt and pepper to taste. Cook, turning the pieces occasionally, until golden, about 15 minutes. Tip the pan and spoon off the fat.

2. Pour the vinegar over the chicken and bring to a simmer. Scatter the celery, capers, and rosemary around the chicken.

3. Cover and cook, turning the pieces occasionally, about 20 minutes or until the chicken is tender and most of the vinegar has evaporated. If there is too much liquid left at the end of the cooking, transfer the chicken pieces to a serving dish. Raise the heat and boil the liquid until reduced.

4. Transfer the chicken to a platter. Tip the pan and skim off the fat with a large spoon. Add a little water and scrape the bottom of the pan with a wooden spoon. Pour the juices over the chicken and serve immediately.

Roman-Style Chicken

Pollo alla Romana

Makes 4 servings

Marjoram is an herb used frequently in Roman cooking. It tastes something like oregano, though much more delicate. If you don't have marjoram, substitute a pinch of oregano or even thyme. Some Roman cooks embellish this dish by adding sweet peppers sautéed in olive oil to the skillet just before the chicken is done.

2 ounces thickly sliced pancetta, chopped

2 tablespoons olive oil

1 chicken, about 3½ pounds, cut into 8 serving pieces

Salt and freshly ground black pepper

2 garlic cloves, finely chopped

1 teaspoon dried marjoram

½ cup dry white wine

2 cups peeled, seeded, and diced tomatoes, or chopped canned tomatoes

1. In a large skillet over medium heat, cook the pancetta in the olive oil until golden brown, about 10 minutes.

2. Pat the chicken dry with paper towels. Add the chicken to the skillet and sprinkle with salt and pepper to taste. Cook, turning occasionally, until the pieces are browned on all sides, about 15 minutes.

3. Tip the pan and skim off the excess fat with a large spoon. Sprinkle the chicken with garlic and marjoram. Add the wine and cook 1 minute. Stir in the tomatoes and bring to a simmer. Cook, stirring occasionally, until the juices run clear when the chicken is cut in the thickest part of the thigh, 20 to 30 minutes. Serve hot.

Chicken with Vinegar, Garlic, and Hot Pepper

Spezzatino di Pollo alla Nonna

Makes 4 servings

My grandmother taught my mother to make this simple spicy Neapolitan-style chicken, and my mother taught me.

Don't even think of using a sweet vinegar like balsamico for this recipe. A good wine vinegar will give the authentic flavor. It won't be too sharp; cooking mellows the vinegar and all the flavors balance beautifully.

1 chicken (about 3½ pounds)

2 tablespoons olive oil

Salt

4 large garlic cloves, finely chopped

½ teaspoon crushed red pepper, or to taste

⅔ cup red wine vinegar

1. Trim off the chicken wing tips and tail. With a large heavy knife or cleaver, cut up the chicken at the joints. Cut the breasts, thighs, and legs into 2-inch chunks. Rinse the pieces and dry well.

2. In a skillet large enough to hold all of the chicken in a single layer, heat the oil over medium heat. Add the chicken pieces without crowding. If there is too much chicken to fit comfortably in one pan, divide the chicken between two pans or cook it in batches.

3. Cook until browned, turning occasionally, about 15 minutes. When all of the chicken is browned, tip the pan and spoon out most of the fat. Sprinkle the chicken with salt.

4. Scatter the garlic and crushed red pepper around the chicken pieces. Add the vinegar and stir, scraping up the brown bits on the bottom of the pan with a wooden spoon. Cook, stirring the chicken and basting occasionally, until the chicken is tender and the liquid is thickened and reduced, 15 minutes. If it becomes too dry, add a little warm water.

5. Transfer the chicken to a serving dish and pour the pan juices over all. Serve hot.

Tuscan Fried Chicken

Pollo Fritto alla Toscana

Makes 4 servings

In Tuscany, both chicken and rabbit are cut into small chunks coated with a tasty batter, then deep-fried. Often, wedges of artichokes are fried at the same time and served alongside.

Tuscans use a cut-up whole chicken for this recipe, but I sometimes make it with just chicken wings. They cook evenly and everybody loves to eat them.

1 chicken (about 3½ pounds), or 8 to 10 chicken wings

3 large eggs

2 tablespoons fresh lemon juice

Salt and freshly ground black pepper

1½ cups all-purpose flour

Vegetable or olive oil for frying

1 lemon, cut into wedges

1. Trim off the wing tips and tail if using a whole chicken. With a large heavy knife or cleaver, cut up the chicken at the joints. Cut the breasts, thighs, and legs into 2-inch chunks. Separate the wings at the joints. Rinse the pieces and dry well.

2. In a large bowl, beat the eggs, lemon juice, and salt and pepper to taste. Spread the flour on a sheet of wax paper. Line a tray or trays with paper towels. Preheat oven to 300°F.

3. Stir the chicken pieces into the egg mixture until well coated. Remove the pieces one at a time and roll them in the flour. Tap off the excess. Place the pieces on a rack until ready to cook.

4. Heat about 1 inch of oil in a large deep skillet or wide saucepan over medium heat. Test to see that the oil is hot enough by dropping in some of the egg mixture. When it sizzles and browns in 1 minute, add enough chicken pieces to fit comfortably in the pan without crowding. Fry the pieces, turning occasionally with tongs, until crisp and browned on all sides and the juices run clear when the chicken is pierced in the thickest part, 15 to 20 minutes. As the pieces are done, transfer them to the paper towels to drain. Keep warm in a low oven while frying the remaining chicken.

5. Serve hot with lemon wedges.

Chicken with Prosciutto and Spices

Pollo Speziato

Makes 4 servings

I had this sautéed chicken dish when I was in the Marches region. The chicken is not browned first, though it does turn out nicely colored. The spices and herbs give the chicken a lively, complex, and unusual flavor and it is very simple to cook.

1 chicken (about 3½ pounds), cut into 8 serving pieces

¼ pound imported Italian prosciutto in one piece, cut into narrow strips

6 whole cloves

2 sprigs fresh rosemary

2 fresh sage leaves

2 bay leaves

1 garlic clove, thinly sliced

½ teaspoon whole black peppercorns

Salt

½ cup dry white wine

1. Arrange the chicken pieces skin-side down in a large heavy skillet. Scatter the prosciutto, cloves, rosemary, sage, bay leaf, garlic, peppercorns, and salt to taste over the chicken. Add the wine and bring it to a simmer over medium heat.

2. Cover the pan and cook 20 minutes. Add a little water if the chicken seems dry. Cook, basting the chicken occasionally with liquid in the pan, 15 minutes more or until the juices run clear when the chicken is pierced with a knife in the thickest part of the thigh.

3. Uncover and cook briefly until the liquid is reduced slightly. Discard the bay leaf. Serve hot.

Chicken in the Style of the Hunter's Wife

Pollo alla Cacciatora

Makes 4 servings

I think I could write a whole book of chicken recipes called alla cacciatora. *One explanation for the name is that chicken, until the last 50 years or so, was a special occasion dish in most homes and not eaten every day. But during the hunting season, the hunter's wife would prepare a chicken to fortify her husband for the rigors of the hunt.*

There are so many variations to this dish. Southern Italians make it with tomatoes, garlic, and peppers. In Emilia-Romagna it has onion, carrot, celery, tomatoes, and dry white wine. In Friuli–Venezia Giulia, it is made with mushrooms. The Genoese make it simply with tomatoes and local white wine. This Piedmontese version is a classic.

2 tablespoons olive oil

1 chicken (about 3½ pounds), cut into 8 serving pieces

2 medium onions, chopped

1 celery rib, chopped

1 carrot, chopped

1 red bell pepper, thinly sliced

1 yellow bell pepper, thinly sliced

½ cup dry white wine

4 ripe tomatoes, peeled, seeded, and chopped, or 2 cups canned tomatoes

6 fresh basil leaves, torn into bits

2 teaspoons chopped fresh rosemary

Salt and freshly ground black pepper

1. Heat the oil in a large skillet over medium heat. Rinse and pat the chicken pieces dry. Cook the chicken, turning the pieces frequently until browned on all sides, about 15 minutes. Transfer the chicken to a plate. Tip the pan and skim off all but 2 tablespoons of the fat.

2. Add the onions, celery, carrot, and peppers to the skillet. Cook, stirring occasionally, until the vegetables are lightly browned, about 15 minutes.

3. Return the chicken to the skillet. Add the wine and bring to a simmer. Stir in the tomatoes, basil, rosemary, and salt and pepper to taste. Bring to a simmer and cook, turning the chicken pieces occasionally, until the chicken juices run clear when the thigh is pierced in the thickest part, about 20 minutes. Serve hot.

Chicken with Porcini

Pollo con Funghi Porcini

Makes 4 servings

In Piedmont, you will see people selling freshly picked porcini mushrooms from makeshift stands at highway rest stops and in parking lots. Because porcini season is brief, these plump wild mushrooms are often dried to preserve all of their heady flavor and aroma. They are not inexpensive, but a little goes a long way. Packaged dried porcini make great gifts—including for yourself. I buy big bags full, which keep a long time in a sealed container.

$\frac{1}{2}$ cup dried porcini mushrooms

1 cup warm water

1 tablespoon unsalted butter

2 tablespoons olive oil

1 chicken (about 3$\frac{1}{2}$ pounds), cut into 8 serving pieces

Salt and freshly ground black pepper

1 cup dry white wine

1. Soak the mushrooms in the water for 30 minutes. Remove the mushrooms and reserve the liquid. Rinse the mushrooms under cold running water to remove any grit, paying special attention to the ends of the stems where soil collects. Chop the mushrooms coarsely. Strain the mushroom liquid through a paper coffee filter into a bowl.

2. In a large skillet, melt the butter with the oil over medium heat. Pat the chicken dry and place the pieces in the pan. Brown the chicken well on all sides, about 15 minutes. Sprinkle with salt and pepper.

3. Tip the pan and skim off the excess fat with a spoon. Add the wine to the skillet and bring to a simmer. Scatter the mushrooms over the chicken. Pour the mushroom liquid into the pan. Partially cover and cook, turning the pieces occasionally, until the chicken juices run clear when the thigh is pierced in the thickest part, about 20 minutes.

4. Transfer the chicken to a serving platter. If there is a lot of liquid left in the pan, raise the heat and simmer until it is reduced and thickened. Pour the sauce over the chicken and serve immediately.

Chicken with Olives

Pollo al'Olive

Rome is the capital of Italy, and people from all over the country gravitate there because of its importance as the center of government, religion, and (to a lesser extent) business. Many of the city's restaurants are run by non-Romans, and the food is sometimes a reflection of the merging of regional styles. I had this chicken in a trattoria in Trastevere, the bohemian neighborhood across the Tiber from the historic center that is popular with the city's young people. Judging by the amount of garlic in the dish, I suspected that there was a southern hand in the kitchen, but I was not able to find out for sure.

2 tablespoons olive oil

1 chicken (about 3½ pounds), cut into 8 serving pieces

Salt and freshly ground black pepper

4 garlic cloves, lightly crushed

½ cup dry white wine

2 tablespoons white wine vinegar

1 cup Gaeta or other mild, flavorful olives, pitted and coarsely chopped

2 anchovy fillets, chopped

1. In a large skillet, heat the oil over medium heat. Pat the chicken pieces dry and place them in the pan. Sprinkle the pieces with salt and pepper. When the chicken is golden brown on one side, after about 10 minutes, turn the pieces, then scatter the garlic all around them. Cook until nicely browned, about 10 minutes more. Remove the garlic if it becomes dark brown.

2. Add the wine and vinegar and bring to a simmer. Scatter the olives and anchovies all around. Partially cover the pan and turn the heat to low. Cook, turning the pieces occasionally, until the chicken is tender and the juices run clear when the thigh is pierced in the thickest part, about 20 minutes.

3. Remove the chicken to a serving platter. Tip the pan and skim off the fat. Spoon the sauce over the chicken. Serve hot.

Chicken Livers with Vin Santo

Fegato di Pollo al Vin Santo

Makes 4 servings

Vin santo is a Tuscan dessert wine made by partially drying trebbiano grapes on straw mats before pressing them to make a very concentrated wine. The wine is allowed to age in sealed wood casks until it turns a beautiful amber color and develops an aromatic, nutty flavor and smooth texture. It is a perfect wine to sip after a meal or to accompany nuts, plain cookies, or cake. Vin santo is also used for cooking—in this case, with chicken livers in a delicious buttery sauce.

Marsala can be substituted for the vin santo. Serve these livers over boiled or fried polenta or slices of toasted bread.

1 pound chicken livers

3 tablespoons unsalted butter

Salt and freshly ground black pepper

1 teaspoon chopped fresh sage leaves

4 thin slices imported Italian prosciutto, cut crosswise into slivers

2 tablespoons vin santo or Marsala

2 tablespoons chopped fresh flat-leaf parsley

1. Trim the chicken livers, cutting away the connecting fibers with a sharp knife. Cut each liver into 2 or 3 pieces.

2. In a large skillet, melt 2 tablespoons of the butter over medium heat. Rinse and pat the liver pieces dry and add them to the skillet. Sprinkle with salt and pepper. Add the sage and prosciutto. Cook, turning the liver pieces frequently, until lightly browned yet still pink in the center, about 5 minutes. Transfer the livers to a plate with a slotted spoon.

3. Add the vin santo to the pan and raise the heat. Bring to a simmer and cook 1 minute or until slightly reduced. Remove from the heat and stir in the remaining butter and parsley. Pour the sauce over the liver and serve immediately.

<u>WHOLE CHICKEN AND CAPON</u>

Roasted Chicken with Rosemary

Pollo Arrosto

Makes 4 servings

Before the 1950s, most Italians lived and worked on farms owned by wealthy absentee landowners. At certain times of the year, usually holidays, the farmers would be expected to pay the landowner a portion of their profits, usually in the form of livestock, produce, wheat, wine, or whatever was produced on the farm. In the Veneto, specific items traditionally were associated with certain holidays. Hens were given at Carnevale, which precedes Lent. Chickens were given for the feast of Saint Peter on June 29, geese for All Saints' Day, November 1. Eggs were the gift for Easter and a suckling pig for Saint Martin's Day on November 11. A roasted chicken dinner was a rare feast for the average person, and even today makes a meal seem like an occasion.

Roasting a chicken breast-side down helps to keep the white meat juicy and cooks the bird evenly. For best flavor, use an organically raised chicken.

This is the most elemental of roasted chicken recipes and, in my opinion, the best. The chicken cooks at a low temperature for the entire time. Scatter some potatoes or other root vegetables, like carrots or onions, around the chicken, if you like.

1 chicken (3½ to 4 pounds)

2 garlic cloves, halved

4 tablespoons olive oil

Salt and freshly ground black pepper

2 or 3 sprigs fresh rosemary

1 lemon, halved

1. Place a rack in the center of the oven. Preheat the oven to 350°F. Oil a roasting pan large enough to hold the chicken.

2. Rinse the chicken well and pat it dry. Rub the skin all over with the garlic. Brush with oil and sprinkle inside and out with salt and pepper. Tuck the garlic and rosemary inside the chicken. Squeeze the lemon juice over the chicken. Place the lemon halves inside the chicken cavity. Tie the legs together with kitchen string. Place the chicken breast-side down in the pan.

3. Roast the chicken 30 minutes. Baste the chicken with the accumulated juices. Continue to roast 20 minutes more.

Carefully turn the chicken breast-side up and roast, basting occasionally, 30 minutes. The chicken is done when the juices run clear when the thigh is pierced and the temperature in the thickest part of the thigh is 170°F on an instant-read thermometer. If the chicken is not browned enough, turn the heat to 450°F for the last 15 minutes of cooking.

4. Transfer the chicken to a platter. Cover loosely with foil and keep warm for 10 minutes before carving. Serve hot or at room temperature.

Roasted Chicken with Sage and White Wine

Pollo Arrosto alla Salvia

Makes 4 servings

The method for this roast chicken is different from the <u>Roasted Chicken with Rosemary</u> *recipe. Here the chicken roasts at a higher temperature, which saves some time and gives the skin more color. Wine and lemon juice transform chicken pan juices into a little sauce for the chicken.*

1 chicken (3½ to 4 pounds)

4 large garlic cloves

Small branch of fresh sage

Salt and freshly ground black pepper

1 small lemon, thinly sliced

2 tablespoons olive oil

½ cup dry white wine

2 tablespoons fresh lemon juice

1. Place a rack in the center of the oven. Preheat the oven to 450°F. Oil a roasting pan large enough to hold the chicken. Place a roasting rack in the pan.

2. Place the garlic, sage, and lemon slices inside the cavity. Rub the oil over the skin and sprinkle with salt and pepper. Tuck the wingtips behind the back of the chicken. Tie the legs together with kitchen string.

3. Place the chicken on the rack in the pan. Roast 20 minutes. Pour the wine and lemon juice over the chicken. Roast 45 minutes more, basting occasionally with the pan juices. The chicken is done when the juices run clear when the chicken thigh is pierced and the temperature in the thickest part of the thigh is 170°F on an instant-read thermometer.

4. Transfer the chicken to a platter. Cover loosely with foil and keep warm for 10 minutes before carving. Serve hot with the pan juices.

Chicken in the Style of Roast Pig

Pollo alla Porchetta

Makes 4 to 6 servings

In central Italy, porchetta *is a whole pig roasted on a spit with fennel, garlic, black pepper, and rosemary. But that is not a dish that is easily made at home, so cooks adapt those same complementary flavors to smaller cuts of pork, rabbit, fish, and poultry. When I first tasted this recipe at the home of winemakers in Umbria, it was made with a guinea fowl, which is similar to a large chicken but with more flavor. A large roasting chicken works just as well. You can use whole fennel seeds in this recipe, or substitute fennel pollen, which is ground up fennel seeds, available at some specialty stores.*

2 large garlic cloves, finely chopped

2 tablespoons rosemary leaves, finely chopped

1 tablespoon fennel seeds or fennel pollen

Salt and freshly ground black pepper

2 tablespoons olive oil

1 large chicken (about 5 pounds)

1. Place a rack in the center of the oven. Preheat the oven to 450°F. Oil a roasting pan just large enough to hold the chicken.

2. Very finely chop together the garlic, rosemary, and fennel seeds. Put the seasonings in a small bowl. Add salt and a generous grinding of black pepper. Add 1 tablespoon oil and stir to combine.

3. Rinse the chicken and pat dry. Tuck the wing tips behind the back. With your fingers, loosen the skin around the breast and legs. Insert half the herb mixture evenly under the skin of the chicken. Put the remainder inside the cavity. Tie the legs together with kitchen string. Brush the skin with the remaining oil. Place the chicken breast side up in the pan.

4. Roast for 20 minutes. Reduce the heat to 375°F. Roast 45 to 60 minutes. The chicken is done when the juices run clear when the thigh is pierced and the temperature in the thickest part of the thigh is 170°F on an instant-read thermometer.

5. Transfer the chicken to a platter. Cover loosely with foil and keep warm for 10 minutes before carving. Serve hot or at room temperature.

Roasted Chicken with Marsala and Anchovies

Pollo Arrosto alla Catanzarese

Makes 4 servings

Giuseppe, an acquaintance in New York, told me that he was originally from Calabria. When I told him that I was planning to visit Catanzaro in that region, he said that I must be sure to visit a type of rustic restaurant known as a putica *to eat* morzello. *He explained that a* putica *is a humble eatery that often has no sign outside, just a large loaf of ring-shaped bread known as a* pitta *mounted near the door. Inside there are large communal tables, and everyone is served an individual pitta filled with morzello, a stew made from cut-up pieces of tripe and other innards. The name comes from* morsi, *meaning "bites."*

My plans changed, and I never did get to Catanzaro, but I do enjoy making this roast chicken that Giuseppe told me his grandmother used to make for holidays and special occasions. The combination of anchovies, Marsala, and chicken flavors may seem unusual, but the anchovies melt down, adding only a salty richness to the chicken juices, while the Marsala adds a nutty flavor and helps the chicken turn a beautiful golden brown.

1 chicken (3½ to 4 pounds)

Salt and freshly ground black pepper

½ lemon

2 tablespoons unsalted butter

8 anchovy fillets, chopped

¼ teaspoon freshly ground nutmeg

½ cup dry Marsala

1. Place a rack in the center of the oven. Preheat the oven to 450°F. Oil a roasting pan just large enough to hold the chicken.

2. Rinse the chicken and pat dry. Tuck the wing tips behind the back. Sprinkle inside and out with salt and pepper. Place the lemon half, butter, anchovies, and nutmeg inside the cavity. Place the chicken in the pan breast-side down.

3. Roast the chicken 20 minutes. Carefully turn the chicken breast-side up and roast 20 minutes more. Pour the Marsala over the chicken. Roast 20 to 30 minutes more, basting 2 or 3 times with the pan juices. The chicken is done when the juices run clear when the thigh is pierced and the temperature in the thickest part of the thigh is 170°F on an instant-read thermometer.

4. Transfer the chicken to a platter. Cover loosely with foil and keep warm for 10 minutes before carving. Serve hot.

Stuffed Roasted Capon

Cappone Ripene al Forno

Makes 6 to 8 servings

For Christmas dinner in the Lombardy region, stuffing for roast capon is traditionally pork sausage and fresh or dried fruit. Mostarda—a variety of fruits, such as figs, tangerines, apricots, cherries, citron, and peaches, jarred in a mustard-flavored syrup—is the typical accompaniment.

Capons, which are castrated roosters weighing 8 to 10 pounds, are generally available fresh around the holidays and frozen the rest of the year. They are meaty and juicy, with a flavor like chicken, only more intense. A large roasting chicken or small turkey can be used for this recipe, but you will need to adjust the cooking time according to weight.

8 ounces day-old Italian or French bread, crusts removed and torn into pieces

½ cup milk

1 pound plain pork sausage, casings removed

10 pitted prunes, chopped

2 large eggs, beaten

$\frac{1}{4}$ teaspoon freshly grated nutmeg

Salt and freshly ground black pepper

1 capon (about 8 pounds)

2 tablespoons olive oil

2 tablespoons chopped fresh rosemary

$\frac{1}{2}$ cup dry white wine

1. In a large bowl, soak the bread in the milk 15 minutes. Then, remove the bread, discard the milk, and squeeze the bread to drain off the excess liquid. Place it back in the bowl.

2. Add the sausage, prunes, eggs, salt and pepper to taste, and nutmeg and mix well.

3. Place a rack in the center of the oven. Preheat the oven to 350°F. Oil a roasting pan large enough to hold the capon.

4. Rinse the capon and pat dry. Lightly stuff the bird with the sausage mixture. (Any leftover stuffing can be baked at the same

time in a buttered baking dish.) Mix together the oil, rosemary, and salt and pepper to taste. Rub the bird all over with the mixture. Place the bird breast-side down in the pan.

5. Roast 30 minutes. Pour the wine into the pan. After another 30 minutes and every half hour thereafter, baste the bird with the accumulated juices. When the bird has roasted 60 minutes, carefully turn the bird breast-side up. Roast a total of 2 hours and 15 minutes, or until an instant-read thermometer inserted in the thickest part of the thigh measures 180°F.

6. Transfer the capon to a platter. Cover lightly with foil for 15 minutes to keep warm.

7. Tip the pan and skim the fat from the pan juices with a large spoon. Carve the capon and serve with the juices and stuffing.

DESSERTS AND COOKIES

Semolina Cookies

Canestrelli

Makes 36

Canistrelli means "little baskets." Crisp and buttery, these Ligurian cookies are made with semolina, which gives them a creamy color and slightly gritty texture.

Semolina is pale gold, hard durum wheat that has been ground so that it has a sandlike texture. Semolina can be fine or coarse. Fine semolina is often labeled semolina flour or pasta flour. It is typically used to make bread, especially in Sicily, and certain types of pasta and gnocchi, such as the Roman Semolina Gnocchi. Semolina can be purchased in many supermarkets, natural food stores, and ethnic markets or from mail order sources.

1²⁄₃ cups all-purpose flour

¹⁄₂ cup fine semolina

¹⁄₂ teaspoon salt

1 cup (2 sticks) unsalted butter, at room temperature

¹⁄₂ cup confectioner's sugar

1 large egg

1. In a large bowl, sift together the flour, semolina, and salt.

2. In a large bowl with an electric mixer, beat the butter on medium speed until light and fluffy, about 2 minutes. Add the sugar and beat until well blended, about 1 minute more. Beat in the egg until blended.

3. Add the dry ingredients and stir on low speed until just blended. (Do not overmix.) Gather the dough into a ball and wrap in plastic wrap. Refrigerate 1 hour up to overnight.

4. Preheat the oven to 350°F. Grease 2 large baking sheets.

5. On a lightly floured surface, with a rolling pin, roll out the dough to a 9-inch circle about $^1/_4$ inch thick. With a cookie or biscuit cutter, cut the dough into 2-inch circles. Place on the prepared baking sheets about 1 inch apart.

6. Have ready 2 wire cooling racks. Bake 13 minutes or until the cookies are lightly golden around the edge.

7. Transfer the baking sheets to the cooling racks. Let the cookies cool 5 minutes on the baking sheets, then transfer them to the wire racks to cool completely. Store in an airtight container up to 2 weeks.

Vin Santo Rings

Ciambelline al Vin Santo

Makes about 4 dozen

Vin santo is a Tuscan dry dessert wine. It is usually served as an accompaniment to dipping cookies, but here it is the principal flavoring ingredient in ring-shaped biscuits. They are made with olive oil and do not have any eggs or butter. The vin santo gives the cookies a subtle wine flavor, while the texture is tender and crumbly. The recipe was given to me by the cook at the Selvapiana winery in Tuscany.

2½ cups all-purpose flour

½ cup sugar

½ cup extra-virgin olive oil

½ cup vin santo

1. Preheat the oven to 350°F. Have ready 2 large ungreased baking sheets.

2. In a large bowl, with a wooden spoon, combine the flour and sugar. Add the oil and wine and stir until smooth and well blended. Shape the dough into a ball.

3. Divide the dough into 6 sections. Cut one section into 8 pieces. Roll each piece between your palms into a 4 × $1/2$–inch log. Shape the log into a ring, pinching the edges together to seal. Repeat with the remaining dough, placing the rings 1 inch apart on the baking sheets.

4. Have ready 2 wire cooling racks. Bake the rings 20 minutes or until golden brown.

5. Transfer the baking sheets to the racks. Let the cookies cool 5 minutes on the baking sheets, then transfer them to the wire racks to cool completely. Store in an airtight container up to 2 weeks.

Marsala Cookies

Biscotti al Marsala

Makes 4 dozen

The warm, sunny flavor of Marsala enhances these Sicilian cookies. Either dry or sweet Marsala can be used. Be sure to serve these with a glass of the same wine. They are similar to the Vin Santo Rings at left, though the texture is lighter and crisper because of the eggs and baking powder, and they are glazed with sugar.

2½ cups all-purpose flour

2 teaspoons baking powder

1 teaspoon salt

1 cup sugar

½ cup dry or sweet Marsala

2 large eggs

¼ cup extra-virgin olive oil

1 teaspoon pure vanilla extract

1. Preheat the oven to 375°F. Grease 2 large baking sheets.

2. In a large bowl, sift together the flour, baking powder, and salt. Pour $^1/_2$ cup of the sugar into a small bowl and $^1/_4$ cup of the Marsala into another.

3. In a large bowl, whisk the eggs and the remaining $^1/_2$ cup of sugar until well blended. Beat in the remaining $^1/_4$ cup of Marsala, the oil, and the vanilla extract. With a wooden spoon, stir in the dry ingredients. Knead briefly until well blended and shape the dough into a ball.

4. Divide the dough into 6 sections. Cut one section into 8 pieces. Roll each piece between your palms into a 4 × $^1/_2$–inch log. Shape the log into a ring, pinching the edges together to seal. Repeat with the remaining dough.

5. Dip the top or bottom of each ring first in the wine, then in the sugar. Place the rings sugar-side up and 1 inch apart on the prepared baking sheets. Bake 18 to 20 minutes, or until golden brown. Have ready 2 wire cooling racks.

6. Transfer the baking sheets to the racks. Let the cookies cool 5 minutes on the baking sheets, then transfer them to the wire racks to cool completely. Store in an airtight container up to 2 weeks.

Sesame Wine Biscuits

Biscotti di Vino

Makes 2 dozen

Only slightly sweet, with a spicy spike from black pepper, these Neapolitan biscuits are good for snacking with a glass of wine and some cheese.

2½ cups all-purpose flour

½ cup sugar

1½ teaspoons baking powder

1 teaspoon salt

1 teaspoon freshly ground black pepper

½ cup dry red wine

½ cup olive oil

1 egg white, beaten until foamy

2 tablespoons sesame seeds

1. Preheat the oven to 350°F. Have ready 2 large ungreased baking sheets.

2. In a large bowl, stir together the flour, sugar, baking powder, salt, and pepper. Add the wine and olive oil and stir until well blended.

3. Shape the dough into a ball. Divide the dough into 4 pieces. Shape each piece into a 10-inch log. Flatten the logs slightly. Brush with the egg white and sprinkle with the sesame seeds.

4. Cut the logs into $3/4$-inch pieces. Place the pieces 1 inch apart on the baking sheets. Bake for 25 minutes, or until lightly browned.

5. Have ready 2 large cooling racks. Transfer the baking sheets to the racks. Let the cookies cool 5 minutes on the baking sheets, then transfer them to the racks to cool completely. Store in an airtight container up to 2 weeks.

Sesame Cookies

Biscotti Regina

Makes 48

Sicilians call these regina, or "queen," cookies because they are so highly esteemed. Though they are rather plain looking, their toasty sesame flavor is addictive. One invariably leads to another.

Look for fresh, unhulled sesame seeds in ethnic markets and natural food stores. These cookies were originally made with lard. Sicilian cooks today often use margarine, but I prefer a combination of butter for flavor and vegetable shortening for tenderness.

4 cups all-purpose flour

1 cup sugar

1 tablespoon baking powder

1 teaspoon salt

½ cup (1 stick) unsalted butter, at room temperature

½ cup solid vegetable shortening

2 large eggs, at room temperature

1 teaspoon pure vanilla extract

1 teaspoon grated lemon zest

2 cups unhulled sesame seeds

½ cup milk

1. Preheat the oven to 375°F. Grease and flour two large baking sheets or line them with parchment.

2. In a large electric mixer bowl, stir together the flour, sugar, baking powder, and salt. On low speed, stir in the butter and shortening a little at a time until the mixture resembles coarse crumbs.

3. In a medium bowl, whisk the eggs, vanilla, and lemon zest. Stir the egg mixture into the dry ingredients until smooth and well blended, about 2 minutes. Cover the dough with plastic wrap and refrigerate 1 hour.

4. Spread the sesame seeds on a piece of wax paper. Put the milk in a small bowl next to the sesame seeds.

5. Take the dough out of the refrigerator. Scoop out a portion of the dough the size of a golf ball and shape it into a log $2^1/_2$ inches long and $^3/_4$ inch wide. Dip the log in the milk, then roll it in the

sesame seeds. Place the log on the baking sheet and flatten slightly with your fingers. Continue with the remaining dough, placing the logs 1 inch apart.

6. Bake 25 to 30 minutes or until well browned. Have ready 2 large cooling racks.

7. Transfer the baking sheets to the racks. Let the cookies cool 5 minutes on the baking sheets, then transfer them to the racks to cool completely. Store in an airtight container up to 2 weeks.

Anisette Toast

Biscotti di Anice

Makes about 3 dozen

Anise, a member of the same family of plants as fennel, caraway, and dill, is considered an aid to digestion. In southern Italy, anise seeds are used to flavor after-dinner liqueurs such as Sambuca and anisette, which gives these cookies their distinctive licorice flavor. For a more pronounced flavor, add a teaspoon of anise seeds to the batter before baking.

2 large eggs, at room temperature

1 tablespoon anisette liqueur or anise extract

$\frac{1}{2}$ cup sugar

1 cup all-purpose flour

2 tablespoons cornstarch

1 teaspoon baking powder

1. Place a rack in the center of the oven. Preheat the oven to 350°F. Grease a 9-inch square baking pan. Line the bottom of the pan with wax paper. Grease and flour the paper. Tap out the excess flour.

2. In a large electric mixer bowl, combine the eggs, liqueur, and sugar. Begin beating the eggs on low speed, gradually increasing the speed to high. Continue to beat the eggs until they are very light and foamy and tripled in volume, about 5 minutes.

3. Place the flour, cornstarch, and baking powder in a fine-mesh strainer. Shake the strainer over the egg mixture, gradually folding in the dry ingredients with a rubber spatula. Be careful not to deflate the eggs.

4. Scrape the batter into the prepared pan and smooth the top. Bake 20 to 25 minutes, or until firm when touched lightly in the center and golden brown. Have ready a large baking sheet and a large cooling rack.

5. Remove the pan from the oven, but leave the oven turned on. Run a small knife around the edges of the pan. Invert the cake onto a cutting board.

6. Raise the oven temperature to 375°F. With a long serrated knife, cut the cake into 3-inch strips. Cut each strip crosswise into $^3/_4$-inch-thick slices. Place the slices in a single layer on a large baking sheet. Bake the slices 7 minutes or until toasted and golden.

7. Remove the cookies from the oven and transfer to wire racks to cool. Store in a tightly covered container up to 2 weeks.

"S" Cookies

Biscotti Esse

Makes 4 dozen

My husband and I had these lovely butter and spice cookies in Milan, where I spent ten days researching an article for the Wine Spectator magazine on the city's best restaurants.

3 cups all-purpose flour

1 tablespoon baking powder

$\frac{1}{2}$ teaspoon salt

$\frac{1}{2}$ teaspoon ground cinnamon

$\frac{1}{4}$ teaspoon ground cloves

$\frac{1}{4}$ teaspoon ground allspice

$\frac{1}{2}$ cup (1 stick) unsalted butter, at room temperature

1 cup sugar

3 large eggs, beaten

2 teaspoons pure vanilla extract

1. Sift together the flour, baking powder, salt, and spices onto a piece of wax paper.

2. In a large electric mixer bowl, beat the butter with the sugar on medium speed until light and fluffy, about 2 minutes. Beat in the eggs one at a time. Add the vanilla and beat until well blended, about 1 minute more

3. Stir in the dry ingredients. Shape the dough into a ball. Wrap in plastic and chill in the refrigerator 1 hour.

4. Preheat the oven to 400°F. Grease 2 large baking sheets.

5. Divide the dough into 2 pieces. Cut each piece into 8. Roll each piece into a $^1/_2$-inch-thick rope. Cut the ropes into 4-inch lengths. Place the lengths in an S shape 1 inch apart on baking sheets.

6. Bake 13 to 16 minutes or until lightly browned. Have ready 2 wire cooling racks.

7. Transfer the baking sheets to the racks. Let the cookies cool 5 minutes on the baking sheets, then transfer them to the wire racks to cool completely. Store in an airtight container up to 2 weeks.

Lightning Source UK Ltd.
Milton Keynes UK
UKHW022012250521
384380UK00002B/237

9 781802 903577